CARDIFF
YESTERDAY

Book Seven

1 (*overleaf*)   The location is Stuart Street and gas lamps, horse-drawn carriages and the Italian ice-cream man combine to bring back a nostalgic whiff of life as it was in Cardiff's Dockland in 1894

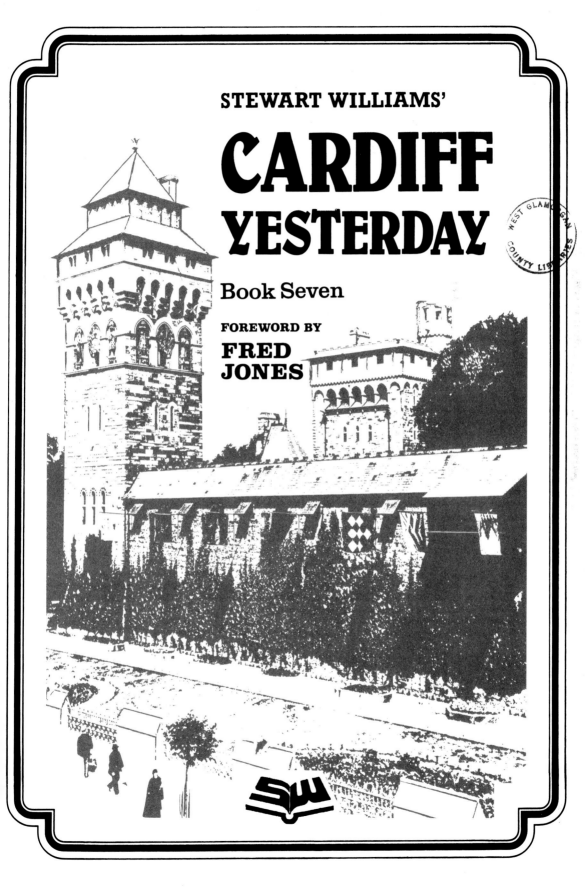

STEWART WILLIAMS'

CARDIFF YESTERDAY

Book Seven

FOREWORD BY
FRED JONES

First published September, 1983

© Stewart Williams, Publishers,
1 Trem-y-Don, Barry,
South Glamorgan

ISBN 0 900807 58 X

ACKNOWLEDGEMENTS

We extend our sincere thanks to the following for kindly giving us permission to use their photographs:—

John F. Andrews (22, 64); Bill Barrett (103, 109, 121, 150, 151, 158, 186, 189, 207); T. J. Bodger (166); D. G. Bowen (77, 83); Cardiff Central Library (1, 2, 3, 4, 6, 7, 8, 10, 11, 14, 15, 16, 19, 20, 21, 28, 31, 32, 33, 36, 37, 41, 48, 49, 61, 62, 63, 70, 78, 91, 97, 100, 104, 133, 134, 135, 136, 137, 181); Mrs Dora Coles (66); Mrs G. Comer (191); Mrs M. Criddle (67, 68); G. A. C. Dart (102); H. Dawe (111); Albert Day (142); Roy Denning (12); Mr & Mrs C. Edwards (116); Miss Reta Gale (99, 129, 130, 131, 132, 138, 210, 211); Mrs Emily Gibson (172); Frank Goddard (120, 122); Glyn Griffiths (113, 163, 164, 183); Perseus Gwyther (161, 175); P. Healan (168); Arthur Hillier (185); W. H. Hughes (153, 154); D. Hutchings (157); Brian James (114); Mrs F. James (101); Derrick Jenkins (144); Miss Barbara Jones (27, 117, 165, 167, 193); Fred Jones (5, 13, 17, 18, 23, 25, 26, 29, 30, 34, 35, 38, 39, 44, 47, 50, 51, 52, 53, 54, 55, 57, 58, 59, 65, 85, 86, 87, 89, 90, 92, 105, 143, 173, 174, 176, 177, 178, 182, 184, 190, 192, 194, 195, 196, 197, 198, 199, 200, 203, 204, 205); Mrs G. M. Jones (9); P. J. Kellaway (118, 123, 128, 162); Mrs Sheila Kite (45); Mrs Sarah Leck (125); Mr & Mrs T. R. Lusty (84, 147, 159); Simon Mansfield (46, 71, 72, 73, 74, 75, 81, 169); Mrs M. Neill (94, 98); I. Norman (40); Mrs Eileen Orpin (24, 80); Nicky Payne (42, 43); Ken Pudge (160); Glyn Rumbelow (115, 155, 156); St Alban's Junior School (171); B. F. Salvidge (188); Mrs Audrey Sawchuck (149); Ken Smitham (112, 187); *South Wales Echo* (201, 202); Cyril Speers (95, 96, 148); Mrs May Stephens (106, 107); Thomas Stephens (56, 108); Bert Street (152); Chris J. Taylor (69, 76); Jack Thomas (170); T. Thomas (60); Mrs L. I. Thompson (126); Mrs Alwyn Tyrrell (88); C. Voyce (82, 127); L. G. Watkins (139, 140, 141); Welsh Folk Museum (79, 206); Mrs Gwen Werner (119, 124); F. C. Wilkie (145, 146, 179, 180).

End papers: Advertisements from *Butcher's Cardiff District Directory 1880-81* in the Fred Jones Collection

Printed in Wales by D. Brown & Sons Ltd., Cowbridge and Bridgend, Glamorgan

Foreword

by FRED JONES

Few Cardiffians of my generation can be unaware of the tremendous interest which has been aroused by the *Cardiff Yesterday* series. The history we learned at school was remote and lifeless—dates, battles and names in endless profusion, but in the pages of these volumes the intimate little reminders of our everyday life become the focus of attention. Buildings, churches, streets and faces strike responsive chords and revitalise memories which had faded almost to extinction.

The value of such a series has been amply demonstrated for me in the way readers have so often contacted me with previously unrecorded information, often of a personal nature, about photographs appearing in *Cardiff Yesterday*. I remember some three years ago I showed Stewart a very nice postcard of a group of Whitsun Treat workers taken at St Fagans in the nineteen twenties (Book 4, No. 84). At first he was luke-warm about it as there was no indication as to which church or chapel the workers were from, or if indeed it was a Cardiff group, although on the back of the card was written 'Whitsun Treat, St Fagans'. When it was eventually published a lady wrote to me from Grangetown saying how thrilled she was to see a lot of her old friends and relations at the St Barnabas Mission Church, North Clive Street, Whitsun Treat.

Another lady from Llandaff contacted me to say that her late uncle was pictured at Albany Road Military Hospital in Albany Road School (Book 3, No. 200) and that he was discharged from the army from there. Another person had two relatives in the Canton Salvation Army Band (Book 2, No. 92). A gentleman from Whitchurch said it was he who was pictured crossing the road by Whitchurch Library (Book 3, No. 27) when a boy, doing errands for his mother. A man rang me from Penarth to say he was the nephew of Mr Morgan of D. Morgan and Son, Windsor Road (Book 2, No. 60). A lady contacted me to say she was a descendant of F. Barter, V.C. of Daniel Street. His homecoming was pictured on a postcard (Book 3, No. 205) with no indication or reference as to what street or, indeed, if it was in Cardiff. We were able to establish the facts and I was able to supply her with a number of other photographs relating to F. Barter, V.C.

Perhaps the most poignant and sad postcard published so far was the funeral of the two Jenkins brothers of Dalton Street. They were both killed in the terrible Senghenydd Disaster of 1913. One gentleman from Cathays told me he remembered the funeral and, indeed, was in a junior class at Crwys Road School when the Jenkins brothers were in another class for older boys. Quite recently I was informed by a friend that three of the nieces of the boys who died still live in Cathays.

My own outstanding memories in the series to date, although they were published out of chronological order, are Book 5, No. 115, Mackintosh Football Club 1899, and Book 4, No. 132, Cardiff City cupwinners 1927. They show Mr Walter Riden as a dapper young man in 1899, and the same man some 25 years later as a director of Cardiff City, 1927. I remembered him some five years later when he was Headmaster of Albany Road School and I a reluctant pupil; remembered him also in the post-war period when Cardiff City rose from the Third Division to the First Division in as many years. I used to catch a tram in City Road to go to Ninian Park and he used to catch the same tram from Penylan Road. We always had a chat on the way to the match; he always rolled his own cigarettes.

In this seventh edition appears another memory for the hundreds of Roath men and women who, as schoolchildren in the 'hungry thirties', daily attended Sirrell's, City Road, for a meal. The postcard is dated 1910 but it remained the same until about 1945 when it was taken over by Astey's as a cafe. Whenever I pass that shop on the corner of Pearson Street it brings back memories, for although fortunately I never attended, I remember dozens of my friends who did. I pass the Gaiety Cinema and still remember the Saturday afternoon matinees. I forget most of the films I saw but remember well the serials—Rex King of the Wild Horses, Galloping Ghost and Lloyd of the C.I.D. and many more.

I remember spending many happy hours watching the aeroplanes over Tremorfa Airport—Alan Cobham with a team of flying aces, and Cardiff Aeroplane Club giving displays throughout the summer. Newport Road from the Power Station to Rumney Bridge, pre-1940, was just a road like a causeway with huge ponds on the one side and open fields on the other. I can remember seeing a flock of sheep being dipped in the Roath Brook just alongside the Transport Depot. As they came out of the brook they shook themselves and ran across Newport Road on the way over Pengam Bridge back to Pengam Farm, with just one man and two dogs in attendance—there was no traffic on Newport Road in those days.

Another interesting photograph in this book is the Dutch Cafe, Queen Street, as it was pre-1914. This picture can be compared with an earlier photograph taken in 1891 (Book 2, No. 14) where one can see the structural alterations made during the earlier years and which remained much the same until 1950 when Halfords took over the premises. The only features visible today on the upper part of Halfords shop are the four Dutchmen plaques. They are also on the Dutch Cafe photograph featured in this volume. One of the many fascinations of these books is comparing one photograph with an almost identical view taken perhaps twenty or more years apart.

I would like to thank Stewart Williams for giving me the opportunity to write a few words and to wish this volume every success, and also to thank all the readers who have written or telephoned me during the time I have been helping with *Cardiff Yesterday*. I should also like to thank the many small photographers and stationers long gone (some to this day are not known by name) who, in their day, captured old Cardiff on film and published postcards to sell at one old penny each, and in some cases a half-penny, and which nowadays fetch such a premium.

Fred Jones

AUTHOR'S NOTE

A glance at the acknowledgements will reveal that Fred Jones has once again provided a large number of interesting photographs, as has been the case since Book 2 was published. It was my good fortune when Fred wrote offering his help after the publication of Book 1 in May 1980. Since that time he has supplied numerous 'gems' from his splendid collection, made valuable suggestions and generally taken a keen interest in the development and success of the series. What more fitting than that he should write the foreword to this book. From it you will quickly gather that, like the rest of us, he is hopelessly hooked on the history of our city. I hope I will continue to enjoy Fred's friendship and support for many books to come and I am glad to pen these few lines of sincere appreciation for all his help.

The accuracy of the captions has added immensely to the value of the books and in this important department I am fortunate indeed to have the support of Geoff Dart, former County Librarian of South Glamorgan. His painstaking research has helped to untie numerous historical knots which seemed to defy all other attempts at solution. Many others too have given unstinted support. Bill Barrett, local historian and baseball expert; Chris Taylor, my transport authority; Bill and Dennis O'Neill, tireless chasers of photographs and ardent supporters; Roy Denning, with editorial help; my cousin Tommy Davies; Con Mullett; Bob Tobin; Doug Kestrell; Cardiff Central Library, whose impressive picture collection has always been most generously made available; the Welsh Folk Museum; the *South Wales Echo* and its editor Geoff Rich who has offered wise counsel and given magnificent coverage in his newspaper; Frank Hennessy and CBC for backing inside and outside the studio; and Bob Whitaker of D. Brown & Sons Ltd., who have printed all my books over the past 25 years.

It is gratifying to know the books are so enjoyed and I value the expressions of appreciation which I regularly receive from all parts of the United Kingdom and overseas. As you know, I am always on the look-out for 'oldies', so if you have anything you think will be of interest please drop me a line. I look forward to hearing from you.

Stewart Williams

1 Trem-y-Don,
Barry, CF6 8QJ

2 Spring sunshine in High Street glimpsed through the main gate of Cardiff Castle, April 1930

3 The fourth Marquess of Bute and his bride inset against a view of Cardiff Castle made a popular post card in the early years of this century. They were married on 6 July 1905

4 New Street looking westward towards the top of St Mary Street. The hoardings screen the Glamorganshire Canal and Mill Lane, *c*.1894

5 Old railway bridge over the Taff, 1908. On the right is Frank's confectionery works in Pendyris Street, Grangetown. The bridge was rebuilt and widened during the reconstruction of the General Station between 1930-34

6 Duke Street looking eastward, showing the north side of the street during demolition in 1923

7 The Duke Street improvement scheme opened up a splendid new view of the castle. It also removed a notorious bottleneck. Here, in 1924, workmen are busy widening the road

8   Traffic weaves its way past the trams as they trundle along the Hayes in 1948

9 The Castle Lodge in North Road was destroyed by a German incendiary bomb in March 1941

10 The *Park Hotel* in Queen Street, *c*.1895. It has been described as 'impressively bulky' and almost a century after being built it still dwarfs most of the surrounding buildings

11/12 The 'Alexander' fountain, now on the feeder bridge in Kingsway, was donated by Wm. Alexander, Mayor 1859-60, and was built into the wall of the St Mary Street Town Hall in 1862 (*see below*). In 1908 it was re-positioned in the wall of the canal bridge at Mill Lane corner (*see left*) opposite the *Terminus Hotel*. When this bridge was removed in 1952 it was rescued and mounted at its present site. The Town Hall view was taken on the occasion of the Coronation of Edward VII in 1902

13 This is how St Mary Street looked in 1910

14 This famous statue by Sir William Goscombe John was stolen from Thompson's Park in 1971 where it had been for 72 years. It was found a year later abandoned near Abergavenny but without its head. It was repositioned in the pond and given a replica head made of fibreglass.

15 The £50 reward poster on the Old Forge at Fairwater refers to a murder which took place on 10 July 1896. The victim was David Thomas, a 35-year-old carpenter. His body was found lying across the path some 100 yards from the Forge. He had been shot twice in the chest. The crime remained unsolved despite wide publicity

16 Grover's Terrace, Mill Road, Ely, c.1900. Montague Grover was Town Clerk of Cardiff, 1864-67

17　Cowbridge Road, Canton, *c*.1915

18　Moorland Gardens, *c*.1920. Behind the striped shelters is Splottlands Branch Library. The land for garden and library was given by the Splott landowner Lord Tredegar

19/20 Seasonal contrasts in these 1891 views of the 200-year-old Llandaff Bridge. Shortly afterwards it was widened and the stone parapets replaced by the lattice ironwork which remained until the recent demolition and replacement of the bridge

21 Tudor Street, Riverside. Its residential and business character has changed considerably since this was taken in 1920

22 Ryder Street, Canton, before the First World War. The name of the street indicates Bute land. Ryder is the family name of the Earls of Harrowby, related to the Butes through Frances Coutts Stuart, one of the two children of the first Marquess by his second wife Frances Coutts

23 A pre-First World War view of Clare Street, Riverside

24 Clare Road, Grangetown, 1912. A supermarket now occupies the church site

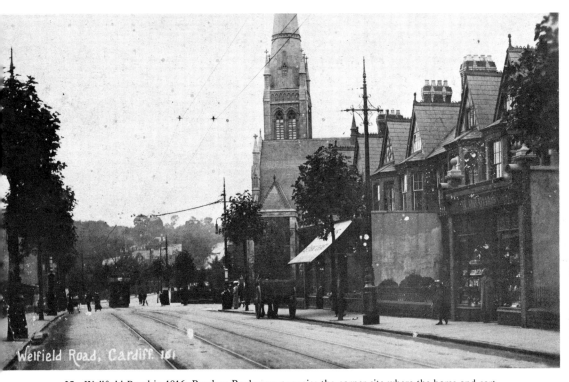

Welfield Road, Cardiff. 161

25 Wellfield Road in 1916. Barclays Bank now occupies the corner site where the horse and cart stand

26 Apart from the tram lines, which have now gone, Whitchurch Road (despite the misleading caption), with Gladstone School on the left and Cathays Branch Library on the right, looks much the same as it did in 1916

Crwys Road, Cardiff. 290.

Lock Cottage, Melingriffith, Whitchurch, Cardiff. 128.

27 This is how Melingriffith looked in 1920. The Glamorganshire Canal is now filled in, the Melingriffith stack has disappeared along with Lock Cottage, but Oak Cottage (beneath stack) is still standing and occupied

28 Whitchurch Library and Velindre Road, c.1912. In the background, behind the tree, is the Mental Hospital which was opened in 1910

29 Whitchurch Golf Links, 1933. The present dual carriageway follows almost exactly the road shown here which was the approach from the north to Whitchurch Railway Station

30 Newport Road, Rumney, 1932. The *Carpenter's Arms* and the entrance to Rumney Court are on the right

31 This ancient milestone, photographed in 1891, is preserved in situ in the triangular garden of Roath Branch Library. On plate 33 (*opposite*) just the top can be seen near the apex of the rough land now the library garden. It seems to read FROM THE TOWN HALL IN CARDIFF 1 MILE. This would be the High Street Town Hall demolished in 1861

32 September 1892 and horse trams rattle along Newport Road. This shows the junction with Broadway. Blanche Street and the *New Dock Tavern* are on the right

33 The original four elms at the junction of Newport Road and Broadway in 1897. Although long gone the name is perpetuated in Four Elms Road and the *Four Elms* hotel. The building in progress on the right is the Trinity Methodist Church, opened in 1897. The triangular site accommodates the Roath Branch Library (opened 1901) and its garden

34 Newport Road between Clifton Street and Roath Court in the early years of this century

35 This attractive framed post card was one of a series published by Stephens, Duke Street Arcade. It shows Newport Road with, on the right, 'Sherwood' the home of Archibald Hood, a prominent coal owner. It was demolished and replaced by Telephone House in the late 1960s

Newport Road, Cardiff.

36 Roath Mill, an 18th-century building, was located near Blenheim Road. This was taken seven years before it was demolished in 1897

37 The opening of Roath Park on 20 June 1894 was an occasion for celebration. This procession of horse-drawn floats is making its way along Wellfield Road

38/39　Rural Rumney as it was before and just after the First World War. (*Above*) The *Rompney Castle* in 1909; (*below*) Orchard Terrace (now Wentloog Road) in the 1920s with the chimney stacks of the *Rompney Castle* prominent in the distance

40 North Church Street, Docks, with St Mary's Church vestry on the left, in 1953

41 Taff Vale Railway Company's bridge across the Taff from Ferry Road, Docks, to Ferry Road, Grangetown (*left background*), built in 1866. The decision of the TVR to levy tolls in 1886 led to the building of Clarence Bridge in 1890 higher up the river. The central portion of the old bridge seems to have been demolished in the mid-90s but vestiges of the long wooden connection stages on either side could still be seen until recent floodworks

42/43 Dockland memories from the 1950s. Stuart Street (*above*) and Dudley Street (*below*), now swept away as part of the South Butetown redevelopment scheme

Trade and Industry

44 For many years Boyles' footwear shops were well-known in Cardiff. These premises, seen in the 1920s, were located at 63 Albany Road, a site later taken over as part of the original Littlewoods stores which was blitzed during the Second World War

45 In the early years of the century travellers staying at the *Queen's Hotel* were collected from the railway station in this coach driven by Thomas George Jones who lived in Grangetown

46 Bread roundsman with horse-drawn van employed by A. E. Richards' City Flour Mills Bakery, Llandaff, *c.*1910

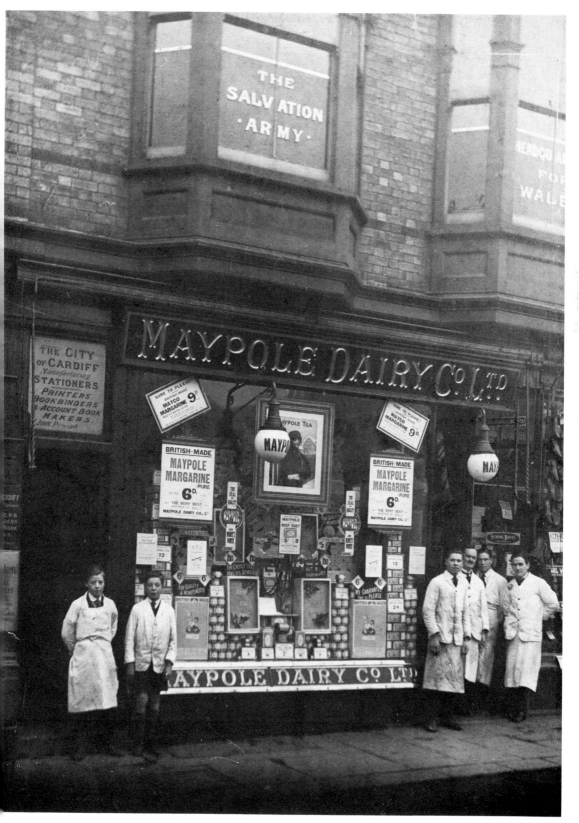

47 The attractive green and gold fascia of the Maypole was a familiar sight in the city and suburbs in the inter-war years. This branch was in The Hayes beneath Stuart Hall, headquarters for Wales of the Salvation Army. Taken in the 1920s

48 R. J. Heath supplied thousands of pianos to generations of Cardiffians. Their shop on the corner of Charles Street and Queen Street (now occupied by Marks and Spencer), here seen in 1910, was a prominent city landmark

49 A busy corner of the Central Market in the early 1900s. Michael Marks (of Marks and Spencer fame) started trading here in 1895

50/51 Trade cards were widely used in the early years of this century. Spillers used the above for general advertisement purposes, while representatives notified shopkeepers of impending calls with the attractive biscuit-bordered card (*below*)

Cardiff, _____ 190 _____

Our Mr. _____ will have the pleasure of waiting

upon you on _____ next, the _____ inst., when the

favour of your esteemed Orders will oblige.

Spillers Nephews, Ltd.

52 The Dutch Cafe in Queen Street was for many years a popular rendezvous for Cardiffians. This was taken in 1916 before the stained glass windows (*opposite*) were fitted. They were removed when Halfords took over the premises in 1950

DUTCH CAFÉ, CARDIFF.

53 Hundreds of Roath schoolchildren now in their fifties will remember the Pearson Street side door of Sirrell's, the bakers, in City Road where in the 1930s they went daily for a free meal. Sirrell's were in business for some 30 years until 1932 when Hunt's took over. Later Astey's bought it and opened a cafe, the Silver Lounge

City Road, Cardiff.

By.T.W. ATTWOOD. ←DESIGNED ~~AND~~ EXECUTED BY T. WILLIAMS, ROSE STREET, CARDIFF.

By.T.W. ATTWOOD. ←DESIGNED ~~AND~~ EXECUTED BY T. WILLIAMS, ROSE STREET, CARDIFF.

54/55 These delightful stained glass windows were designed by T. W. Attwood and made by T. Williams in his Rose Street, Roath, workshop. They were incorporated into the front windows of the Dutch Cafe in the early 1930s

If you suffer from

INDIGESTION, CONSTIPATION, MUSCULAR RHEUMATISM, NEURITIS, SCIATICA, &c.,

— Try —

PETERSON'S

CONSULTATIONS FREE.

VAPOUR BATHS,
ELECTRIC MASSAGE,
and
PHYSICAL EXERCISE.

It will put you right.

Hours—10.0 a.m. to 8.0 p.m.

Ladies' Days:
TUESDAY and FRIDAY,
10.0 a.m. to 2.0 p.m.

Telephone No. **4359.**

Peterson's Health Institute Ltd.

6 & 7, St. John Square, Cardiff.

J. T. HUTCHINS, LIMITED,

SHIP STORE MERCHANTS,

Burt Street, Bute Docks, CARDIFF.

Telegrams: "Lustre, Cardiff."   Telephone **346.**

AGENTS FOR RENOWNED

COLLAN OIL

For all kinds of LEATHER, SPORTING GUNS, AND STEEL GOODS.

58   J. T. Hutchins was one of many ship store merchants carrying on business in the Docks area
during the 1920s when this advertisement appeared

SESSIONS & SONS, LTD., CARDIFF
(Also MANCHESTER & GLOUCESTER).
WINNERS OF GOLD MEDALS.
MANUFACTURERS AND IMPORTERS OF EVERY KIND OF MATERIAL USED FOR BUILDING PURPOSES.

59 Sessions' premises in Penarth Road extended from Trade Street to the Kardov building. It was destroyed by enemy action *c*.1941

60 This was Navigation Paint Company's entry in the 1934 'Trade Pageant'. The vehicle was a Ford

61 Roath Power Station, 1927

62 The *White Swan* in Shakespeare Street was demolished in March 1972. Many remember the large white swan painted on the roof of the building. During the Second World War the authorities had it painted black as it was thought to be a good landmark for enemy aircraft

63 Women, many from Newtown, worked as dockers during the early years of this century. These gangs are seen unloading potatoes at England's wharf

64 Cardiff and District motor traders' visit to Fort Dunlop, 12 April 1935

65   Arlington, a London company, came to Cardiff in 1931 and opened a garage at 2 Westgate Street. They moved to Dumballs Road in the late 30s and will also be remembered in Newport Road (on the site now occupied by Allied Carpets) where they sold coaches and commercial vehicles

66   Elliott Equipment staff outing, 1938. Their parachute factory was in Collingdon Road, West Dock, and later they opened a barrage balloon factory in East Dock. Due to bomb damage their work was removed to James Howell's premises in St Mary Street where they stayed for the duration of the war

67/68 The Brooks family for three generations served the Marquess of Bute as gamekeepers and for much of this time lived in the Lower Gate Lodge in Sophia Gardens. Isaac William Brooks (*left*) was gamekeeper from 1860-1900; his son William (*right*) lived in a Bute property at Leckwith where he reared pheasant and partridge for the Marquess. In 1911 he returned to the Lodge where the family remained until 1925 when they moved to the Upper Lodge off Cathedral Road. Their work consisted of protecting game and the peacocks in the Castle grounds and checking licences to curb poaching of fish in the Taff. William died in 1952; his widow lived on at the Lodge until her death in 1972 aged 92

69 This 1911 Commer 36 hp 34-seater double-decker of Cardiff Tramways Co. Ltd., was used on the Cardiff-Whitchurch service. The vehicle had a narrow body giving longitudinal seating downstairs

70 A Cardiff Tramways Company solid-tyred Dennis double-decker outside Whitchurch Post and Telegraph Office in 1910

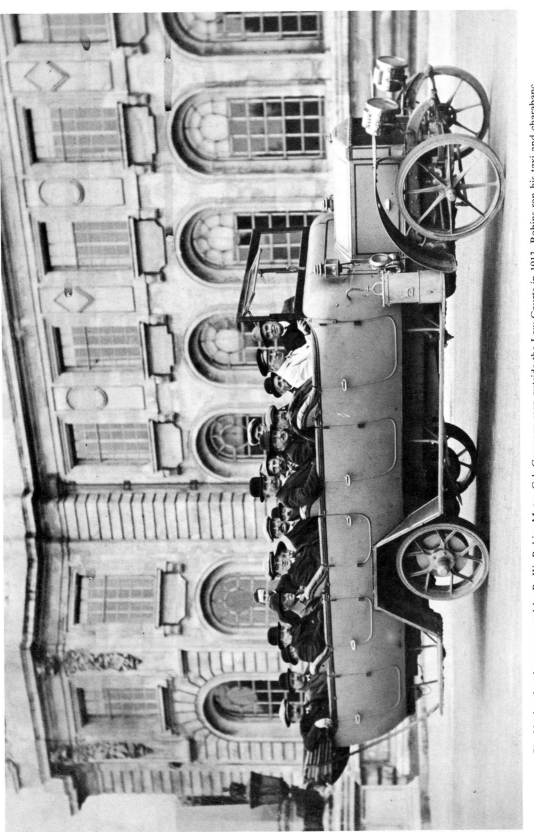

71   Napier charabanc operated by R. W. Robins Motor Cab Company seen outside the Law Courts in 1913. Robins ran his taxi and charabanc
business from the Institute Garage (opposite the New Theatre) in Greyfriars Road. He discontinued trading in 1920

72 Daimler luxury coach in 'silver cloud' livery operated by C. J. Vincent & Sons, 2 Corporation Road, Grangetown. New in April 1930

73 This open-top Leyland Tiger coach *c.*1930 was bought from Woods of Blackpool by H. J. Cridland & Sons, Paget Street, Grangetown, who retained the original 'seagull' livery of grey, black and cream

74 Splott Liberal Club about to depart on their annual outing in September 1914. The Daimler charabanc was operated by Cardiff Tramways Company

75 All we can add to the detailed caption on this trade card is the date—1919

76 This AEC Regent 50-seater was Cardiff's first oil 'bus. Delivered new in July 1932, it was operated on trial until 1934 when the Council finally decided to switch from petrol to oil

77 In order to provide outings for the disabled the City Council bought this vehicle from Western Welsh in September 1960 and modified it to enable wheelchairs to be loaded

78 (*opposite*) Solomon Andrews' Llandaff 'bus stands at its starting point outside Cardiff Castle whilst a horse-drawn tram passes on its way to Canton. The 'bus would carry about 26 passengers and the tram about 40. For many years the Llandaff 'buses ran at half-hourly intervals in both directions

79 Andrews' Llandaff horse 'bus en route from the terminus outside the Castle to the *Black Lion* at Llandaff, 1900. The route ran via Castle Street, Cowbridge Road, Wyndham Crescent, Severn Road (now Severn Grove), Mortimer Road, Conway Road and Penhill, where a 'cock' horse was used in the ascent

80 Hancock's drays were once a common sight in Cardiff, but this 'fine team of greys' was used mainly for show purposes

A FINE TEAM OF GREYS
used by Messrs Wm.
HANCOCK & Co. Ltd.
The Cardiff Brewers

81 This open-top tram was one of a batch of 20 built by Dick Kerr and bought in 1902 for £540 each. It worked the Clare Road Depot-St Mary Street-Clarence Road route

82 Tram derailment outside Albert Hagon's chemist shop in Hayes Bridge Road, November 1938

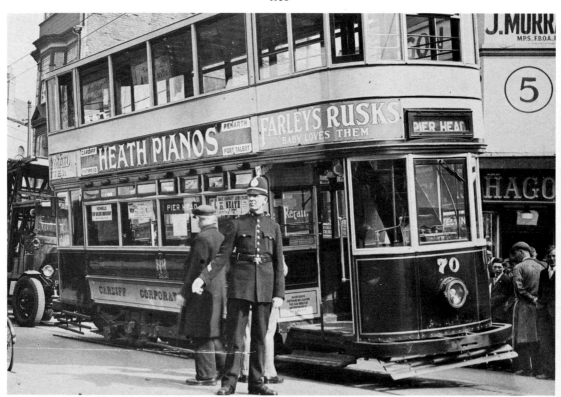

83 The end of an era—taking down a Transport Department sign in Mill Lane after the withdrawal of trolley-bus services to the Pier Head in January 1964

84 The donor's father, Gordon Lusty (*right*) lost a g in the First World War, but this did not prevent im from driving a taxi for T. G. Page whose garage as situated alongside the *Halfway Hotel* in Cathedral Road when this was taken in 1920

"Perfect in every Part."

THE HIGHEST form of Engineering skill, backed by every resource of Science and Capital, is. brought to bear on the design and construction of the

WOLSELEY-SIDDELEY
AUTOCARS.

(Proprietors - VICKERS, SONS & MAXIM, Ltd,)

Every component part is submitted to the most stringent tests. For Reliability, Silence, and Low Running Costs, Wolseley-Siddeley lead the world.

LOCAL AGENTS:

PERRY & TURNER, LTD.,

Motor Agents and Carriage Builders,

Telephone—P.O. 394, Cardiff.
Telegrams—" Carriages, Cardiff."

Frederick St., CARDIFF.

Also at STOKES CROFT, BRISTOL.

85 Few could afford the luxury of a motor car in 1909 but for those who could this Wolseley-Siddeley had much to offer. Cardiff agents Perry & Turner Ltd., placed this advertisement in the commemorative book of the National Pageant of Wales held in Cardiff 26 July to 7 August 1909

86 Rhymney railway bridge, carrying the GWR main line over the river Rhymney, the morning after a German air raid in the Second World War. The New Road area can be seen in the top left corner

87 A Foden 'over type' steam wagon operated by Fredk. J. Sparks & Son, the Cardiff haulage contractors, in 1913, seen in their South William Street yard

Religion, Education and Public Service

88 Opening of New Trinity Sunday School, on the corner of Cowbridge Road and Theobald Road, by Lady Bennett, wife of Sir Ernest Bennett, MP for Cardiff Central, in 1934

Tabernacle C.M. Church, Whitchurch, Glam.

89 Tabernacle Calvinistic Methodist Church (now called Whitchurch Presbyterian) in Merthyr Road, 1920

90 Wesleyan Church, Whitchurch, 1910. In 1911 it was rebuilt and extended to the Penlline Road frontage. It is still located in the angle formed by that road and Kelston Road on the south side of the library roundabout. It is now called the Methodist Church

Wesleyan Church, Whitchurch, Nr Cardiff

91 St Martin's, Albany Road, in 1920. The elaborately painted interior was destroyed in the blitz
and the church was restored in 1955

92 Bread and tea for the needy distributed by members of the Salvation Army and Boy Scouts
outside Gladstone School, *c.*1910

93 Longcross Street Baptist Church outing in the mid-1920s

94 Oddfellows' Parade passing the City Hall in 1934

95/96 Charabanc outings in the 1920s were something to look forward to with keen anticipation and most churches and chapels organised trips for Sunday School scholars and adult worshippers. Wesley Methodist Church, Grosvenor Street, Canton, was no exception, although just how many eventually got away in the bottom picture only the photographer knows!

97 The bread roundsman is emerging from Roath Village School house in 1894. The school was situated alongside Roath Court in Albany Road

98 Grangetown Board School, *c.*1897

99 Using a chair as a rostrum the headmaster addresses a full gathering of pupils and parents in the yard at Roath Park School on Empire Day, 1909

100 St John's National School, 1912. This building stood across and at right angles to what is now the Friary

101 Cardiff Pupil Teachers' Centre, 1913-14

102 St Peter's Infants' School, Roath, sailors' hornpipe group taking part in a concert for parents in the school annexe at 9 Richmond Crescent in 1925

103 A Gladstone School class in the 1920s

104 Radnor Road School prize day, 1921-22. The Lord Mayor (Alderman Harold Turnbull) poses with a group of prominent pupils

105 Skerry's College, Newport Road, 1910. This block was demolished to make way for the Welsh National School of Medicine

106 Tredegarville School, 1920. The teacher is Miss Cotton

107 Metal Street School, 1919. An unusual instance of a church school known by a street name. Later known as St German's National School

108 Tredegarville School, 1920

109   Herbert Thompson Infants' School, 1924.

110   Albany Road School, 1926

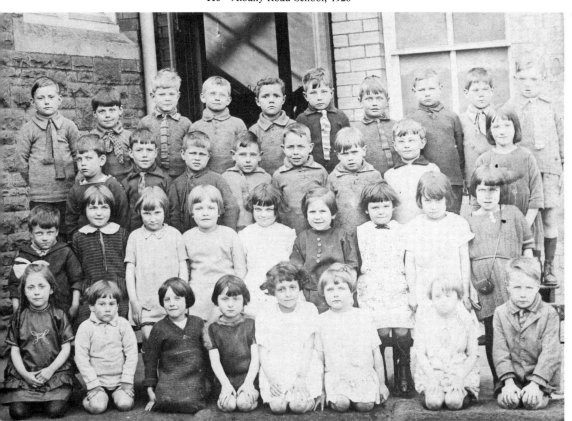

111 Herbert Thompson Infants' School, 1930

112 Birchgrove Junior School, Standard 4, 1936

113 Moorland Road School, Standard 2, 1937

114 Moorland Road School, *c*.1939

115 Gladstone School, Standard 6, 1938. Fifth from left in the second row from the back is Stan Stennett, the well-known show business celebrity

116 Wentloog Junior School, Rumney, 1939

117   Gladstone School, *c*.1946

118   Standard 4, Herbert Thompson School, Ely, 1951

119 Hawthorn Road Infants' School, Llandaff North, St David's Day celebration, 1949

120 A happy souvenir of their stay at Porthcawl Camp in 1953 for these Ely youngsters

Windsor Clive Sec Mod Girls. Porthcawl Camp. Oct. 1953.

121 A party from the Central Boys' Club on an international exchange visit to Osnabruck, West Germany, in 1952. The leader, Bill Barrett, is in the front (*centre*)

122 Windsor-Clive School, Ely, (Juniors), 1958

123 Form 2, Fitzalan Technical High School, 1953. Taken at Howard Gardens before the school moved to new premises at Broad Street, Leckwith

124 Hawthorn Road Junior School, Llandaff North, 1958

125 Standard 3a, Cwrt-yr-ala Junior School, Ely, 1960

126 Roath Park Junior School, Standard 4, 1960-61

127 Members of Cardiff City Fire Brigade and Police march along High Street in the Lord Mayor's Church Parade, 1925

128 'A' Division, No. 20 Fire Force, attached to the Royal Ordnance Factory, Llanishen, with some of their trophies won in fire fighting competitions, *c*.1941

129/130 In April 1931 Cardiff City Police formed their first 'motor patrol'. It consisted of two cars (Humber and Standard Ensign), two BSA motor cycle combinations, and two Sunbeam motor cycles. (*Above*) A proud moment as members of the Watch Committee inspect the patrol outside the Law Courts; (*below*) PC Gale, one of the city's first motor patrol officers, with the *Church Inn*, Llanishen, in the background

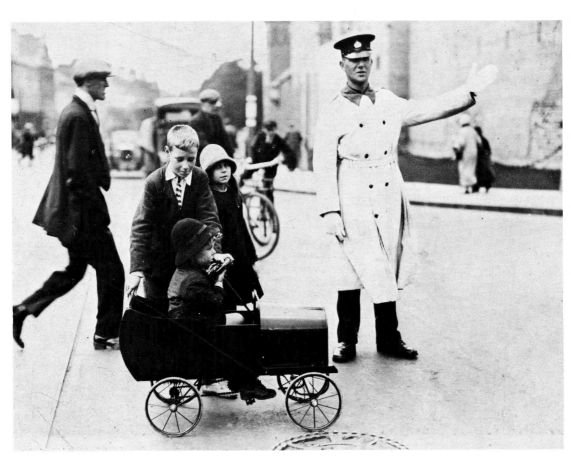

131 Time was when a toddler could cross the busy junction of Duke Street and Kingsway in a pedal car—but that was in 1939. On point duty is PC Gale (see No. 130)

132 A new intake of young police officers pose with their sergeant in the Law Courts yard, *c.*1930

133/134 Cardiff's first municipal hospital, the isolation hospital for infectious diseases (now Lansdowne Hospital) was built at Leckwith in 1895. The aerial view (*above*) was taken in 1935; (*below*) for many years the hospital had to contend with flooding caused by the River Ely over-flowing

135/136 (*Above*) The original Cardiff Infirmary was founded in 1836. This building, built and endowed through the generosity of Daniel Jones of Beaupre, was later occupied by the University College and demolished in 1960. (*Below*) In 1883 it was removed to its present position in Newport Road at the site of Longcross Barracks

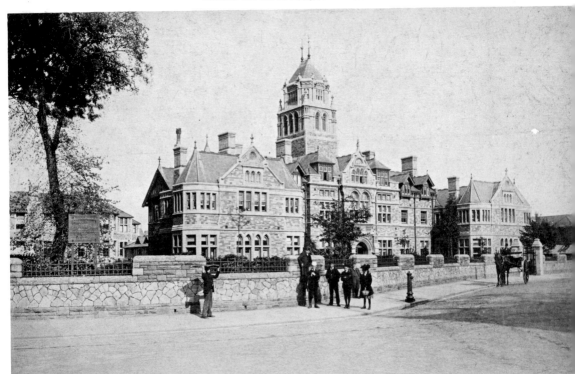

137 The Royal Hamadryad Seamen's Hospital in Ferry Road under construction *c.*1904 with (*left*) part of *SS Hamadryad*, a former man-of-war which served as a hospital ship from 1866 until the present building was opened

138 A fine body of men—Council workmen employed at Roath Park in the 1920s pose by the landing stage

Sport and Entertainment

139 Bala-born Jack Evans was Cardiff City's first professional signing. He joined them for 35/-per week and the promise of an outside job in the printing trade on 7 June 1910 after previously playing for Wrexham where a shoulder injury threatened to end his career. Jack also had the distinction of scoring City's first goal—against Aston Villa in the inaugural match at Ninian Park, although City lost 1-2. A tricky winger with a blockbusting shot, he played eight times for Wales

140/141 Billy Hardy (*in action shot, left*) and Fred Keenor (*right*) are names synonymous with Cardiff City's outstanding soccer achievements in the 1920s, although in these early action pictures, taken in October 1925, they were fighting a desperate rearguard action against a powerful Arsenal side at Highbury in a game which City lost 5-0. Hardy joined City in 1911 from Stockport. A brilliant wing-half, his neglect by the England selectors was thought to be because he played for a Welsh club. Cardiff-born Keenor signed in 1912 and made 32 appearances for Wales

142 Cardiff City FC, 1937-38. (*Back row*) Jimmy Mitchell, Jim Smith, J. Finlay, Jack Elsey, Tommy Williams, Walter Main, Jim McKenzie, Bryn Davies, Cliff Godfrey; (*standing*) Bill Jennings (Manager), Jack Prescott, Bill Bassett, Cecil McCaughey, Les Talbot, George Poland, Bob Jones, Bill Fielding, Ernie Blenkinsop, Eli Mort, Bill Cantor (Asst. Trainer), Eugene Melaniphy, Jack Kneeshaw (Trainer); (*seated*) Lou Ford, Alec Brown, John McCall, George Walton, Chris Page (Chairman), Arthur Granville (Captain), Jim Mellor, Bert Turner, George Nicholson; (*front row*) Ted Smallman, Douglas Gear, Reggie Pugh, Jimmy Collins, Albert 'Dapper' Day, C. J. 'Midge' Hill

143 Cardiff City, 1922-23. (*Back row, left to right*) Jack Nock, Jack Page, Ben Davies, Bert Smith, Fred Stewart (Manager), Billy Turnbull, Joe Clennell; (*middle row*) Billy Grimshaw, Jimmy Gill, Len Davies, Jimmy Blair, Harry Nash, Jack Evans; (*front*) Fred Keenor, Herbie Evans

144 Royalty never received a more rapturous reception than Cardiff City's FA cup winning team when they returned home to Cardiff on 25 May 1927. An estimated 250,000 people cheered the players as they held aloft the trophy on their triumphant journey from the General Station to Cathays Park

145 Welsh schoolboy internationals, 1933-34 (*left to right*) Don Emery (Ely Council), F. C. 'Dixie' Wilkie (Radnor Road) and R. Calnan (Radnor Road), taken at Ely Recreation Ground

146 Radnor Road also excelled at cricket and this team won the Schools' Cup in 1933-34

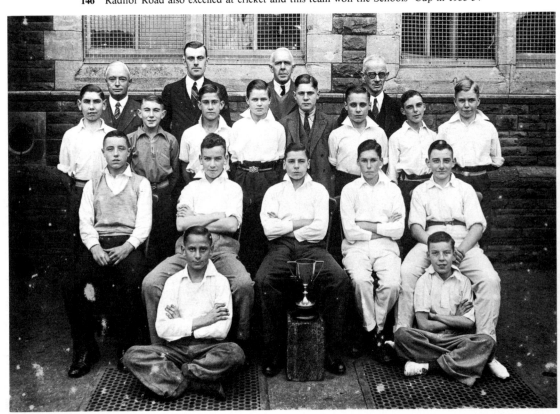

147 Radnor Road School team 1937-38 with Welsh internationals James Butler and Tony Mullett

148 Ely Council School soccer team, 1940. Captain was Gordon Pembrey who played for Cardiff Boys and joined Cardiff City as a professional

149 Moorland Road School soccer team, *c*.1930

150 Moorland Road School team, 1935, containing three future professionals—Billy James (Cardiff City), behind shield, Len Dutton (Norwich City), wearing Welsh cap, and Albert Stitfall (Cardiff City), front left

151 Another impressive Moorland Road team, 1937-38. Captain was Charlie Anderson and Welsh cap Rhys Thomas

152 Severn Road School with an impressive display of trophies won at various sports in 1931-32

153/154 Under the direction of sports master Bob Loosemore Windsor-Clive School won soccer and baseball honours during the 1930s. The schoolboy international (*above*) is W. H. 'Pussy' Hughes who later played professional football for Hartlepool United

155 Gladstone School soccer XI, Schools' League Third Division champions, at Ninian Park in 1937 for their 'glory' cup final against Moorland, which sadly they lost. Glyn Rumbelow was captain

156 Gladstone School soccer team, 1937-38

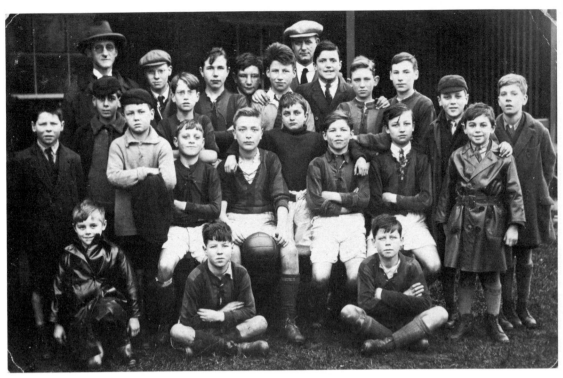

157   Gladstone School soccer team, late 1920s

158   Ely Congregational (Grand Avenue) FC, 1929-30

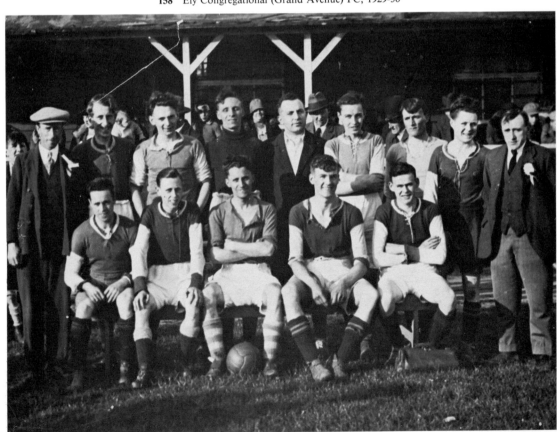

159 Canton FC, a prominent club in local amateur football before the First World War

160 Philog FC, 1924-25. The goalkeeper is Arthur Miles subsequently to become one of Wales' most accomplished water colour artists

161 Roath Villa in the 1920s. Captain was Perseus Gwyther

162 Royal Ordnance Factory, Llanishen, soccer team 1939-40

163 Bridgend Street Juniors soccer team, Splott, in the mid 50s

164 Docks Athletic 1956, members of Cardiff Wednesday League

165 Mackintosh Football Club, 1900-01

166 Players and officials of Penylan Rugby Club during the early years of the century

Penylan F.C. 1906-1907

167 Cardiff RFC Reserves, 1904-05. Captain was D. L. Evans

168 Cardiff Crusaders' RFC, Mallett Cup winners 1928-29. Captain was J. Regan

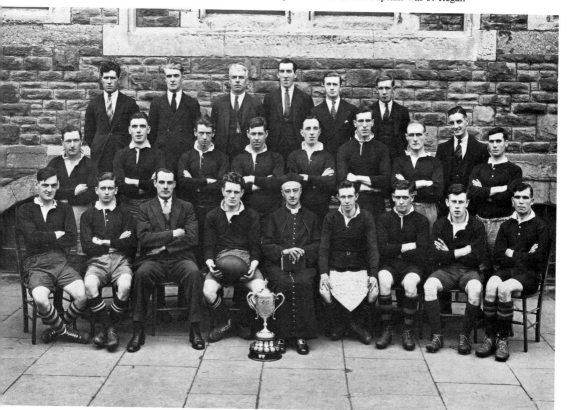

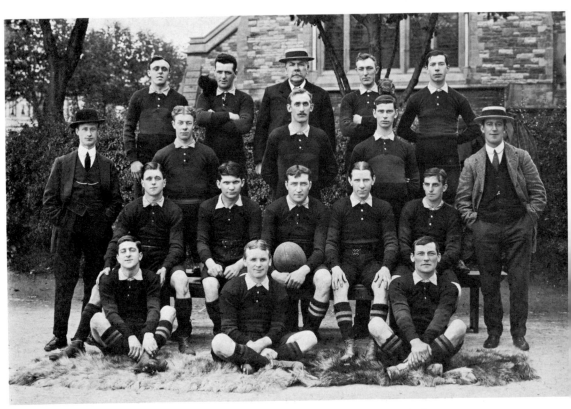

169   Canton RFC, Mallett Cup Finalists, 1912-13. Captain was T. Raynor

170   Grange Baptist RFC 2nd XV, 1919-20. The president, Lieut. H. Turner, MC (a member of
the well-known building family) is seated (*centre*) alongside the captain, G. H. Cornish

171 St Alban's RFC 'Invincible Year' 1932-33. Their record—played 16, won 15, drawn 1, lost 0

172 Ninian Park School rugby XV 1933-34, undefeated Cup and Gibson Shield winners. Captain was James Gibson, later capped as the Cardiff Boys' inside half, who went on to skipper Penarth RFC and played hooker for Cardiff Rugby League Club in 1951

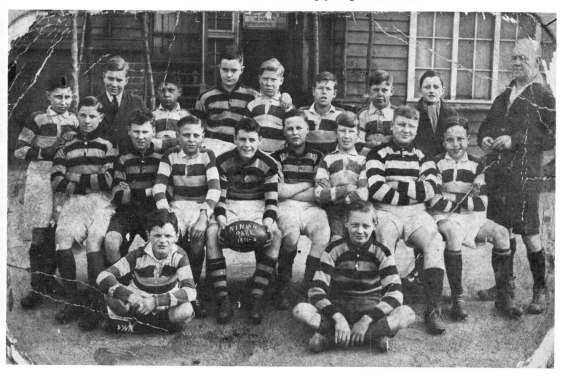

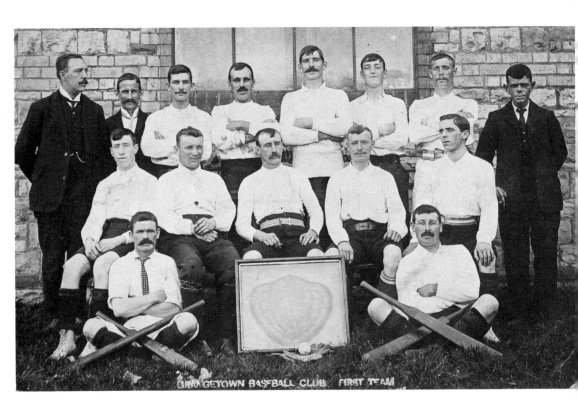

173/174 Grangetown has always produced good baseballers and these 1906 (*above*) and 1907 teams, proudly displaying their trophies, obviously took the game seriously

175　Penylan Baseball Club on an outing to Weston-super-Mare in 1924

176　Penylan baseball supporters involved in an advertising stunt outside the club headquarters, the *Albany* in Donald Street, 1931

177/178   St Peter's, Roath, Water Polo Club. (*Above*) The team at Guildford Crescent Baths; (*below*) members enjoying a bathe at Penarth. Both were taken *c.*1913

179 Elyn Harriers, 1929. Members were employed at Melingriffith Works

180 Gymnastics Club held at Guildford Crescent Baths and run by Mr Sandford

181 Start of a walking race from the *Maltsters Arms*, Llandaff, to Cowbridge Road and back, *c*.1905. Winner was Arthur James who covered the 16 mile course in 2 hours 20 minutes

182 Group in Mount Stuart Square (west side), *c*.1907. The man with the bicycle was a member of Cardiff Jockey Cycling Club which flourished from the early years of the century until the First World War

183 Docks Athletic annual outing to Gloucester

184 St Fagans Cricket and Bowls Pavilion, 1935

CRICKET & BOWLS PAVILION, ST. FAGANS.   9922

185 St Cadoc's RC Junior School, Llanrumney, scored a notable baseball double in 1970 when the girls won the Junior Schools' knock-out cup competition and the boys lifted the Coslett Cup. Sports teachers Anne Head and Arthur Hillier are on the left and headmaster John Buckley is on the right

186 No mistaking the pride on the faces of these St Alban's youngsters who enjoyed a highly successful year in 1959

187 This splendidly turned-out Tramways band poses in the transport yard before a concert

188 Cardiff and District GWR Orchestra, winners of the Challenge Cup, Swindon Musical Festival, 1929

189 St Alban's Silver Band with their conductor John Williams at Cardiff Arms Park in 1952

Floor Staff & Band, American Roller Rink, Cardiff.

190 Roller skating is still a popular pastime, but in 1912 Cardiff could boast of at least three rinks, the biggest and best being the American in Westgate Street

191 Cardiff Madrigal Society, winners at the Royal National Eisteddfod of Wales, 1938

192   Concert parties were a big attraction at Roath Park Pavilion for many years. This was taken in 1916

193   Cardiff Youth Hostel Association Folk Dance Group at the National Eisteddfod, Ebbw Vale, 1958, where they won a folk dance competition

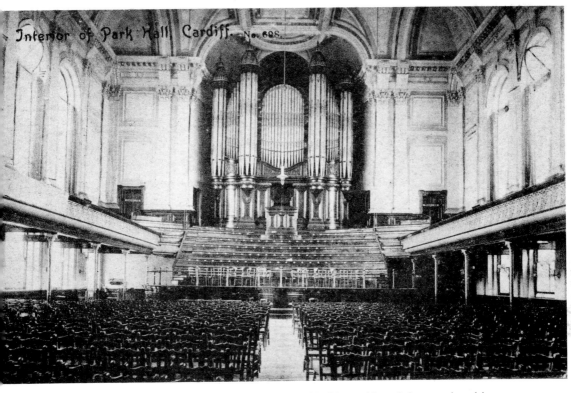

194 The impressive interior of the Park Hall in the 1920s. Many celebrated singers and musicians appeared on stage at this theatre

195 Sixty years ago Uncle Norman, Auntie Betty and Uncle Felix broadcast their children's programmes from Station 5 W.A. in Castle Street. This was the post card they sent to young admirers

CARDIFF
EMPIRE

QUEEN STREET

PROPRIETORS   MOSS EMPIRES, LIMITED.
Managing Director   Mr. FRANK ALLEN
Acting Manager   HERBERT J TAYLOR

MONDAY, JAN. 6th, 1913 and TWICE NIGHTLY
AT 6.45 AND 9.0 DURING THE WEEK

THE WORLD-FAMOUS SELF-LIBERATOR!

HOUDINI

Presenting the Greatest Performance of his Strenuous Career liberating himself
after being Locked in a

WATER TORTURE
CELL

Houdini's own Invention, whilst Standing on his
Head his Ankles Clamped and Locked above in
the Centre of the Massive Cover   A Feat which
borders on to the Supernatural

£200

Houdini offers this sum to
anyone proving that it is
possible to obtain air in
the upside-down position
in which he releases himself from this WATER-
FILLED TORTURE CELL.

CASELLI SISTERS
Vocalists and Dancers

HAPPY TOM
PARKER
COMEDIAN AND DANCER

196   Seventy years after his appearance at the Empire in Queen Street, Houdini is still remembered as the cleverest escapologist of all time

197 D'Arc's Waxwork Exhibition, St Mary
Street, 1913. The girl was a live model.
During the 1930s the same theme was
presented with a wax model

D'ARC'S MARIONETTES AND
D'ARC'S WAXWORK EXHIBITION,
CARDIFF.

198 The resident orchestra at Cox's Cafe, 114 Queen Street, c.1928

MISS FLORENCE HORTON, of Cardiff, scored the highest number of votes in a recent *Daily Sketch* Beauty Ballot. She says :—
" Amami is the best Shampoo I have ever used. It keeps my hair lovely and brings out the tints."

199 A Cardiff pin-up of the 1920s. Sixty years later we wonder what happened to the winsome Miss Horton

200 Fela Sowande became resident organist and pianist at the Capitol when he came to Cardiff in November 1940 with Tommy Handley's ITMA show. An accomplished musician, Sowande toured the world with Jack Hylton's band

201/202 Dan Donovan was a big name in entertainment during the inter-war years. Born in Grangetown, he led a band in Cox's Cafe (where the New Continental now stands) during the 1920s and crooned his way to the top with Henry Hall, regularly broadcasting to an audience of millions. In 1938, when the photograph on the left was taken, he was engaged to sing with his own band at the fashionable Lansdowne Restaurant in Berkeley Square, London, in succession to Brian Lawrence. During the war he frequently entertained Cardiff audiences at Sunday night concerts. Now in his 80s Dan (*right*) relives those wonderful memories through his recorder

SOUVENIR

CARDIFF CASTLE

CITY HALL

VISIT OF
THEIR MAJESTIES
THE KING & QUEEN

VILLA · CARDIFF

TO OPEN
THE NEW IMPORT DOCK
AT CARDIFF JULY 13TH, 1907

BUTE DOCKS

DAVIES (LITHO) LTD. CARDIFF

203 *(opposite)* An enlargement of a coloured souvenir card published in 1907. The reverse side contains a detailed itinerary of this historic Royal visit

204/205 HRH the Prince of Wales on a visit to Cardiff in February 1918. These photographs were taken at the Channel Dry Dock and among the VIPs are the Marquess of Bute and Sir William Tatem (who became Lord Glanely in July that year). The main purpose of the visit was for the Prince to open the Prince of Wales Orthopaedic Hospital, although he also found time to visit the Royal Hamadryad Seamen's Hospital and the Curran factory

206 Prime Minister Ramsay MacDonald visiting the University College of South Wales and Monmouthshire in the 1930s

207 Carlton Restaurant staff about to set out on a day's outing in the 1930s

208/209   This one-man band tootling along Bwlch Road, Fairwater, had a Pied Piper effect on the local children. His identity is a mystery, but the year was 1946

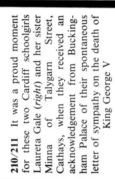

210/211 It was a proud moment for these two Cardiff schoolgirls Laureta Gale (*right*) and her sister Minna of Talygarn Street, Cathays, when they received an acknowledgement from Buckingham Palace of their spontaneous letter of sympathy on the death of King George V